VANISHING
WILDLIFE

Glossary

These categories, except **Threatened**, are drawn from the *Red Data Book* issued by the International Union for Conservation of Nature and Natural Resources (IUCN).

Extinct
Not definitely located in the wild in the past fifty years.

Endangered
In danger of extinction unless the factors affecting them are changed. This category includes species whose habitats have been so drastically reduced that their survival is unlikely. It also includes species that may be extinct, but which have definitely been seen in the past fifty years.

Vulnerable
Likely to move into the Endangered category soon if the causal factors continue to operate.

Rare
Species with small world populations that are not presently endangered or vulnerable, but are at risk.

Threatened
Endangered in part of its range.

Indeterminate
Known to be endangered, vulnerable or rare, but not enough information is available to indicate which category is appropriate.

Out of Danger
Formerly in one of the above categories, but now considered to be relatively secure because effective conservation measures have been taken or causal factors removed.

Insufficiently Known
Suspected to belong in one of the above categories, but not enough information known to make designation.

Introduction

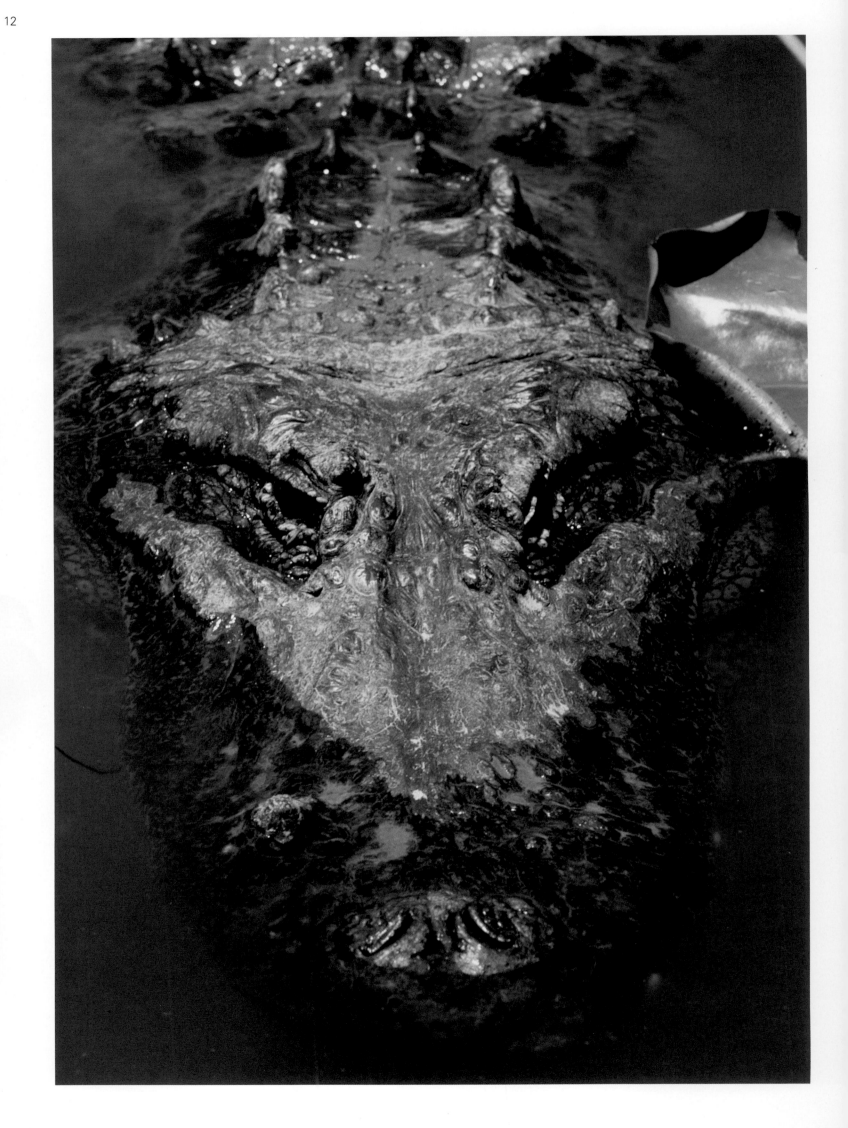

(above)

The passenger pigeon (*Ectopistes migratori-ous*) once blackened the skies of North America. Stuffed specimens like this one, in a museum in Swift Current, Alberta, are all that is left.

(left)

The American alligator (*Alligator mississippi-ensis*), once endangered through overhunting for its hide, and through draining of its marshy habitat, is now classed as out of danger due to successful conservation measures aimed at habitat protection.

(preceding pages)

A number of international conservation organizations, including World Conservation International and the London Zoological Society, are working to count and study the habits of those black rhinoceroses (*Diceros bicornis*) that remain in the wild.

OVER THE COURSE OF MORE THAN 3 BILLION YEARS, LIFE ON OUR great planet has evolved into a spectacular array of plants and animals, each one interrelated and dependent on others in the vast web of life that joins all creatures, including humans, to a common destiny: to live and then to die. The ancient Greeks called our living planet Gaia or Mother Earth. Today the Gaia hypothesis maintains that life itself controls the health and welfare of the earth, the oceans, the land and the air. We cut and alter portions of the giant web at our own risk. Unfortunately, we have been blithely taking that risk for quite some time and the web is showing signs of structural damage.

Mankind has occupied the planet for what amounts to the blink of an eye. During most of that time, we have lived more or less in harmony with the land and the animals. But in the last 100 years of our existence, we have wreaked unparalleled havoc on our fellow inhabitants, relentlessly and thoughtlessly pursuing them to the brink of extinction, and many beyond. In just fifty years we have caused more damage to the living earth than in all our years as a species on this planet. Prior to this century, an average of one species per year was lost to extinction, spanning a period of some 600 million years. Many ecologists believe that today that rate has shot up to several species per day, and there is real fear that by the end of this century the rate could be galloping along at 100 per day (several per hour!). At present rates we stand to lose twenty-five to fifty percent of the species presently on earth by the year 2050. Based on past and present extinction rates, many scientists feel that we are in the midst of a mass extinction. Some say that it could be even greater than the extinction that wiped out the dinosaurs.

The International Union for the Conservation of Nature and Natural Resources (IUCN) has identified a total of some 4,589 animals known to be

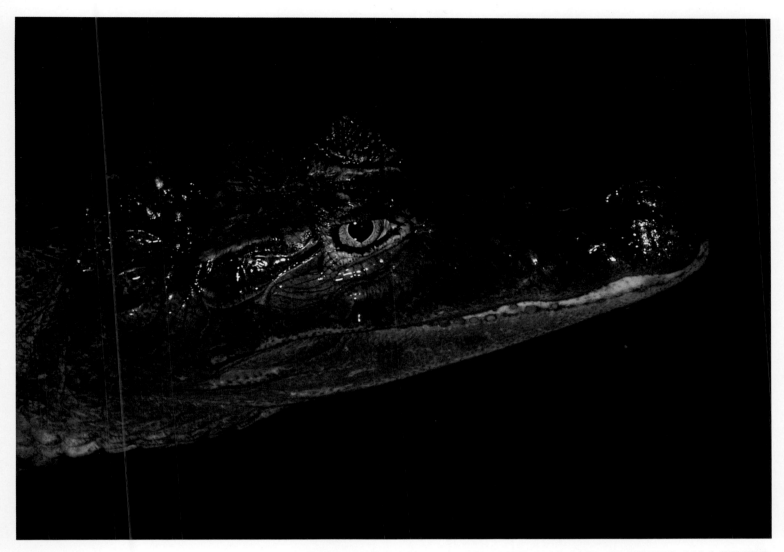

(above)
After killing millions of black caiman in the nineteenth century, hunters turned to the less desirable spectacled caiman (*Caiman crocodilus crocodilus*) of northern South America and the Amazon.

(left)
The palm cockatoo barely survives in its limited range in Papua New Guinea, Indonesia and the Cape York peninsula of northern Australia.

(preceding pages)
The Asiatic lion (*Panthera leo persica*) is restricted to the Gir Forest Sanctuary and surrounding area of western India. It is endangered by habitat loss as lands around the park are turned over to agriculture.

WE ARE MORE THAN 5 BILLION STRONG AND GROWING ON A FINITE planet with finite resources. We are the ultimate carnivore. Our meat-eating habits place us at the top of a food chain that begins with the transfer of energy from the sun, to photosynthetic plants, to animals that eat the plants, to animals that eat animals. We contribute more mass to the world's inventory of living matter than any other species. By the end of the century we may hit 6 billion, an astounding increase of 4.5 billion since 1900. By 2075 we could hit 12 billion. All these humans have specific needs that must be fulfilled in order to survive and needs beyond that pertaining to their quality of life. These needs spell trouble for the other creatures on our planet. They, too, need space but we are pushing them out and destroying their homes. Already, the developed countries have exploited a large part of their resources, draining marshlands, felling forests and damming rivers. Most of Europe's forests have fallen under the ax – England has just eight percent of her forests remaining. So many trees have been felled to fuel the consumer societies that now gaze longingly at the resources of the developing countries.

Nowhere is the destruction happening more quickly than in the world's rain forests. These tropical ecosystems, important enough to affect the climate of the world at large, are located in some of the poorest countries in the world. Though they cover only six percent of the earth's land surface they provide shelter for perhaps fifty percent of the estimated 5 to 10 million species which live in this world. Indeed, these figures are likely conservative, as recent studies have indicated there may be as many as 30 million species on earth! Of those we have only discovered and named some 1.7 million, most of which are invertebrates – critters without backbones. With the destruction of the rain forest proceeding apace, we stand to lose perhaps as much as

secretive giant armadillo and several South American monkeys, including the white-nosed saki, southern bearded saki, and the white marmoset. These are all endangered species that are now exposed to human activity as never before.

Peasants have moved into the region, cut down the trees and burned them to make way for their crops. The lights of their fires show up like thousands

include the habitats for all the avocado species that the bird requires, thus forcing it to move out of the reserves during the relevant seasons.

Animals confined to small reserves are at a great risk of being decimated by disease or natural disaster. The mountain zebra is found only in small reserves in Africa and could be wiped out by disease or drought. The Puerto Rican crested toad is hanging on, but its last few natural breeding ponds are threatened by development and hurricanes. The mountain gorilla's last stronghold is in the Virunga Mountains of Rwanda, Uganda and Zaire. Similarly the giant panda of China is confined to small areas and is doubly at risk because of its specialized diet of bamboo shoots.

Despite the growing number of reserves set aside for wildlife, there is concern that most reserves may be too small to do the job, even assuming that they provide total protection. From the air, the Amazon looks like something skinned alive by one inexperienced with a skinning knife. Huge chunks of vegetation are left behind, while adjoining areas are scraped away. Brazilian law now requires that half the land be left in a natural state. The green chunks that are left behind became the focus of the Minimum Critical Size of Ecosystems Project, the inspiration of Thomas Lovejoy of the World Wildlife Fund. This study aims to discover what happens when animals are forced to leave their clearcut home and seek refuge in so-called "green islands." Island biogeography theory suggests that small, remote islands have a higher rate of extinction and fewer immigrants than bigger islands that lie closer to the mainland. The question is whether the ecology of green islands is likely to follow a similar pattern.

Lovejoy chose an area of the central Amazon, just fifty miles (80 km) north of the city of Manaus, to conduct the research. Authorities of the local government, local cattle ranchers and Brazilian scientists agreed to cooperate. Early results are unsettling. When a habitat that was once continuous is suddenly isolated, species vanish and the habitat itself begins to decay. Many birds are killed immediately because they won't migrate to the sanctuary. Other birds cram into the green islands, causing an initial overpopulation problem and lots of territorial conflicts and competition for space and food. The population in one 2.5-acre (1-ha) area dropped to just one half the original level, ten days after the initial disruption. The composition of the species changed and species' numbers dropped. Even the 250-acre (100-ha) green islands were not large enough to retain most mammals. White-lipped peccaries (a kind of pig), agoutis, jaguars and ocelots simply fled the area. The loss of one species can have a domino effect, and cause problems for all manner of other species that may have depended on it in some way for shelter or food. Because the white-lipped peccary left the area, for example, three species of frog soon vanished. The wallows the pigs made disappeared, and with them went the frogs' breeding areas. The three-toed sloth provides shelter for many species of insect that dwell quite happily in its fur. If the sloth dies out, these insects lose their little world and many may not be able to adjust. The forest itself suffers as well. Trees die more quickly in green islands. Hot, dry winds have easy access to the trees on the edge, affecting their growth and driving out or killing many insects which depend on the trees for shelter. This in turn forces insect-eating birds to leave.

Smaller reserves seem to cause more drastic changes than larger reserves, but early research suggests that most reserves today are too small to protect an area without changing it into something different, thereby defeating the purpose of preserving a habitat type. The minimum size necessary for the

The roseate spoonbill (*Ajaja ajaja*) is the only spoonbill found in North America. Its characteristic bulbous bill enables it to feed on small fish and crustaceans as it sweeps back and forth through the mud of marshes. Widespread drainage of swampland threatens its habitat.

maintanance of an ecosystem and to prevent extinctions may well be in the order of millions of acres. But just where do we find that kind of empty land in poverty-stricken nations?

Animals with nowhere to go inevitably run into trouble with man. Our wildlife is being backed into a corner and some species are lashing back. Elephants in Asia and Africa are having a hard time finding enough grazing land. A population of some 500 Asian elephants may require anywhere from 200 to 2,000 square miles (52 000 to 520 000 ha) of forest, but the forest is shrinking, and is being broken up into parcels by an ever-expanding human population. Hungry elephants, more tolerant of disturbance than many other animals, are now destroying cropland in Asia.

In Africa the situation is the same. Elephants are trampling crops and breaking fences in an attempt to feed themselves. An African elephant may consume up to 500 pounds (227 kg) of fodder per day, or 4,000 tons (3600 tonnes) during its life. It has to find that food in a shrinking world where even the reserves are not always big enough to support them. Other big mammals are suffering from lack of space: rhinos, hippos, cape buffalos, tigers and lions. Many wild ungulates (grazing animals) compete for grazing space with billions of domestic cows, sheep and goats. In South Africa the blue buck and

The Malayan tapir (*Tapirus indicus*) lives in swampy, dense jungle in southeast Asia. This habitat is slowly shrinking as the forests are felled.

the quagga (a member of the horse family) were driven to extinction to make way for cattle. The story is much the same thoughout the African savannah and in other grasslands worldwide. The Przewalski's horse of China became extinct in the wild in the 1950s, its pastureland overrun by domestic livestock. Cattle belonging to the Masai of Africa compete with wild game. During the wildebeest migrations, the Masai are hard-pressed not to take their cattle into the Masai Mara game park. Often they cannot resist the temptation, and their cattle are found there.

The migration patterns of many animals pose problems as well. Wilde-beest, elephant and caribou migrate across national borders and in and out of reserves, passing through areas inhabited by people governed by different laws, and with different attitudes to wildlife. Animals protected in one country may have no protection in another. Migrating birds protected on their nesting grounds in the Northern Hemisphere face large-scale destruction of their habitat in the south. The number of songbirds in North America is dwindling.

Global protection of habitats is crucial to stop the rollercoaster ride to ex-tinction. Governments are beginning to realize that they have an obligation to begin the repairs. It remains to be seen whether we can move over and make enough room for our wildlife.

Soiling the Planet

The eastern bluebird (*Sialia sialis*) is one of a number of indigenous birds that have been pushed from their traditional nesting areas by more aggressive introduced species.

Plastics

Pollution affecting animals is not just chemical. There are many other forms of pollution lurking in the world awaiting unwary animals. Plastic bags and leatherback sea turtles seem an unlikely combination but they are a deadly one. Leatherbacks, the largest marine turtles in the world, are found around the globe, usually in tropical and subtropical waters. They eat jellyfish. Inside their throats they have backward-projecting spines to help keep the jellyfish moving in the right direction. Leatherbacks have been found dead along the eastern coast of the United States and elsewhere, their intestines blocked by plastic bags and other plastic debris. Mistaking the bags for jellyfish, the turtles swallow them and the spines in their throats prevent regurgitation. Even on the high seas these turtles are not safe from the plastic garbage that has contaminated all the oceans of the world. Even the plastic rings holding a six-pack of beer together are murderous nooses for many seabirds who get caught in them and slowly strangle.

Fishing nets

The sea is a busy place. All manner of people, from independent fishermen to large scale fisheries worldwide make their living catching fish, shrimp and other creatures with a wide variety of nets. The nets are strong and durable. Drift nets can be some 25 miles (40 km) long. They are a floating, invisible hazard for marine life which is not the target of the nets, but which gets caught simply because it is there. In the North Pacific, some 20,000 miles (32 000 km) of drift nets are set each night, and this figure may be low. Although figures are hard to get, some authorities say they account for the deaths of 10,000 Dall's porpoise, 50,000 fur seals and 250,000 seabirds every year. Sea otters, harp seals and many other species are also accidental victims of these and other nets. In the normal course of events, many of these nets are discarded or lost and become a drifting menace for years.

In the Labrador Sea, 7,000 cod traps and 300,000 gill nets pose severe problems for fin whales, minkes and, most commonly, humpback whales which become entangled. Instead of being shot as they were in times past, many are now released, but if they are trapped for too long they drown.

Sea turtles, all of which are endangered, die in nets meant for shrimp. Shrimp boats off the eastern coast of the United States and elsewhere, have been dragging their nets for longer and longer runs (because of declining shrimp stocks) and catch many turtles that drown before the nets are brought in. Devices designed to prevent capture of turtles are being used by many shrimpers now and seem to be effective in cutting down deaths.

Tourism

People contribute to the discomfort of animals by their very presence. Some creatures are extremely secretive and highly specialized, and intrusions by man can have disastrous results. Three species of endangered bats – the Indiana bat, gray bat and Virginia big-eared bat – are threatened by tourists and spelunkers who flock to their caves, waking them from hibernation to the point where they no longer have the energy reserves necessary to see them through the winter.

Sea turtles coming up to lay their eggs all along tourist beaches in such

and dogs ate the adult kakapo, and rats ate the chicks. Today the kakapo is threatened with extinction as more predators in the form of ferrets, cats and stoats join the fray.

In Mauritius, the endangered Mauritius kestrel and Mauritius parakeet are threatened by macaques and tree-climbing rats that eat their eggs. The ground nesting dodo went extinct due in part to a lust by humans for its meat, but also because it was easy prey for pigs, monkeys and rats. The endangered Guam rail was nearly sent over the brink by the brown tree snake that arrived on Guam after the Second World War. Until recently, the Guam rail survived only in zoos, but biologists have reintroduced it, not to Guam, but to another island nearby that is free of the snakes.

Gone are the Guadalupe storm petrel, Aukland Island merganser, New Zealand's Stephen's Island wren (one cat sent the entire species over the brink), Choiseul Island crested pigeon, New Zealand laughing owl, Hawaiian rail, Zapata wren of Cuba, some species of burrowing owl, Jamaican wood rail and a host of others, all due to introduced predators and competitors such as cattle, sheep and goats.

The cards seem to be stacked against our wildlife. It is being forced to crowd into smaller and smaller areas which themselves are degraded by pollution and overcrowding. Yet, because we share this planet, the cards are also stacked against us. The difference is that we can do something about it. We have used the world as one big garbage dump, owned by no one and abused by everyone. If we are to stop the cycle of damage we have to look to ourselves and our lifestyle and begin to refuse those products we really don't need. Millions of plastic bags are used to pack groceries, and plastic wrapping is used to package all manner of items. Where there is a choice, choose products that are not packaged in plastic. Take cloth bags to the supermarket and department stores. Ask the sales people to put your purchases in them. A store that uses plastic bags and excess packaging will begin to get the idea that it is not acceptable if enough people complain. Already one supermarket chain in Canada is offering reusable cloth bags for sale to their customers. Try to avoid buying any disposable items that are used once and thrown away, such as styrofoam cups (take your own cup to work), paper plates and disposable diapers. If the demand for environmentally unacceptable products drops, the market will be forced to adjust. Buy environmentally friendly products. Try using biodegradable soap, laundry detergent, shampoo and household cleansers. Buy only soft drinks in cans and bottles that are recyclable. If your town or city has a recycling program, use it. Try to cut down on the use of your automobile and use only unleaded gas. Tell your friends what you are doing and why, and encourage them to do the same. With a concerted effort on the part of every individual we can break the cycle of abuse. It is not yet too late.

The
Business
of Killing

(above)
Goodfellow's tree kangaroo (*Dendrolagus goodfellowi*) of Papua New Guinea does, indeed, sleep in trees. They are vulnerable due to hunting pressures and habitat loss.

(left)
Although the walrus (*Odobenus rosmarus*) is still viable, it was once numerous enough to support a major harvest, and is now clearly in some danger. It has been extirpated in its Canadian range, in the Gulf of St. Lawrence.

Gunter Buch's farm lies 7,000 feet (2100 m) above sea level in the mountains on the western edge of the Amazon River basin. Within his 750 acres (300 ha) stands some of the last virgin forest in the area. For thirty years he has defended it from peasants who, having ravaged the surrounding countryside, turned their attention to Buch's untouched land. In 1975 Buch's wife, Mechthild, was shot and killed by neighbors who had continually cut the Buch's fences to allow their livestock to graze on their land.

In Kenya, twenty-two poachers were killed in 1980 during a battle with the rangers of the Masai Mara Reserve. Fortunately no rangers died. In Tarutao National Park, off the southwestern coast of Thailand, a ranger in training was killed by poachers. Three poachers also died in the shootout. Dian Fossey, the woman whose research on gorillas is world famous, was brutally slain with a *panga* (a machete) in 1985 at her research station in Rwanda, by per-

The poisonous Mexican beaded lizard or Gila monster (*Heloderma suspectum*) is considered to be in some danger in its desert range.

(above right)
The prairie long-tailed weasel (*Mustela frenata longicauda*) is threatened in its southern Canadian range due to loss of its aspen parkland habitat and overhunting for pelts.

Food, wallets and other luxuries

Many other endangered creatures are hunted still. Sea turtles, despite being protected throughout their range, are taken for their shells which are turned into jewelry and other trinkets. Monkeys are hunted for their skins which are turned into rugs, and for their teeth and skulls which become ornaments and jewelry. Cobra and python skins become wallets, boots and belts along with the skins of many species of crocodile and caiman. The boldly patterned skins of many snakes that are traded make them easy for customs officials to identify. Traders are now turning to more nondescript snakes, such as rat and sea snakes, to satisfy the market for snakeskin. Bears are shot so their pelts can be made into rugs and their claws into jewelry. Birds of paradise are taken for their feathers or they are stuffed and mounted. Many mountain gorillas have been killed in the past in order to capture their young for zoos. One of naturalist and conservationist Dian Fossey's gorillas, a dominant male named Digit, was killed as he tried to protect his troupe. His hands and head were cut off and sold as ashtrays and ornaments.

Dealers supplying the exotic food trade kill many creatures. Sea turtles are taken to make turtle soup and their eggs are harvested as a delicacy. Hundreds of millions of birds are captured each year during migration. They're harassed in their nesting sites, taken as pets, eaten or stuffed and mounted. In 1984, two Brazilians were fined and jailed for offering, at a wildlife barbecue, 2,400 songbirds as the main course.

Some people hunt endangered species as trophies for their living room walls; the more endangered the animal, the more desirable it becomes.

The klipspringer (*Oreotragus oreotragus*) is limited to a confined range of rocky outcroppings and cliffs in South Africa.

(above)

The orangutan (*Pongo pygameus*) of Borneo, Sumatra, Indonesia and Malaysia lives primarily in rain forest. Their habitat is being eliminated by lumber interests. In addition, poachers kill mature females to get at their young for the live animal trade.

In Burma it is illegal to export either elephants or ivory unless the elephant is old or unable to work. Although Asian elephants do not have tusks as large as their African counterparts, they are still in demand. Illegal traders hammer rusty or dirty nails into the feet of otherwise healthy elephants, which soon fall lame and ill. They are then allowed out of the country. Traders use the living animal to carry its own ivory out of Burma where it is slaughtered and its tusks removed and sold legally.

The trade in endangered species is now sometimes linked to the trade in drugs with its sophisticated smuggling networks and big money. Heroin and cocaine have been found stuffed into dead toucans, force-fed to snakes and incorporated into laminated floorboards or hidden in secret compartments in cages holding aggressive animals. Cocaine dust has been used to replace the white preservative used on crocodile skins. It is later vacuumed up at its destination.

The illegal trade in endangered species flourishes today despite laws to stop it. The laws are hard to enforce, but while there is little direct action the individual can take to solve the problems of environmental degradation, individuals can have an immediate impact on traffic in dying species by refusing to buy the trinkets, furs and ornaments made from their carcasses.

Epilogue

(preceding pages)
There are eight recognized subspecies of
tiger (*Panthera tigris*). Most, if not all, are
endangered by hide hunters, loss of habitat
and persecution by humans who fear them
or suspect them of killing livestock. Although
legally protected in most of their range,
enforcement is difficult.

(below)

The grizzly bear (*Ursus arctos*) ranges over North America. Those in Canada are not yet considered to be endangered, but it has gradually disappeared from much of its American range. The last grizzly was sighted in California in 1922, and in Oregon in 1953. The Mexican subspecies (*Ursus arctos nelsoni*) is certainly extinct.

(above)

The gray fox (*Urocyon cinereoargenteus*) lives in the forests of North America. Its numbers have declined in areas where trees have been clearcut by logging interests.

PEOPLE ALL AROUND THE WORLD HAVE MOVED INTO ACTION, setting up individual conservation programs to help save from extinction a huge roster of animals, from tigers to whales to pandas. Their work in getting reserves set aside and laws written and enforced has brought a number of animals back from the brink of extinction. The Arabian oryx, California condor, Siberian white crane, Puerto Rican crested toad, woolly spider monkey, peregrine falcon, whooping crane and others owe their continued existence to a whole army of dedicated people who have set up captive breeding programs, the goal of which is to return endangered animals to the wild. The results, in some cases, have been encouraging and the work is admirable, yet these programs are treating just one of the symptoms, not the cause, of the problem.

Homo sapiens. Human beings. People. We are the single biggest threat to